SIMPLE LTC SOLUTION

*How to Protect Your Life's Savings with a
Long-Term Care Partnership Program*

Scott A. Olson, CLTC

Cover designed by Carolyn Olson

Scott A. Olson CLTC
Visit my website at www.LTCShop.com

Printed in the United States of America

First Printing: Mar 2018
Independently Published

ISBN 9781980586371

CONTENTS

CHAPTER 1

THE INSURANCE INDUSTRY DOES NOT WANT YOU TO READ THIS BOOK.

This book gives you knowledge from an insider (me). This knowledge will empower you to make the right decisions and protect your life's savings from long-term care expenses.

The number of long-term care insurance policies has increased from 4.5 million in the year 2000 to over 7.1 million today. However, sales of new policies have declined 14 of the last 15 years. In 2016, only 90,000 new long-term care insurance policies were purchased. There are several reasons for the decline in sales, but there's one main reason:

> *The insurance industry does NOT want you to buy long-term care insurance.*

That's crazy, right? Why wouldn't the insurance industry want you to buy an insurance product? Here's why. There are thirteen companies that sell long-term care insurance (here's the list). There are over 100 insurance companies that sell life insurance. The 100+ companies that sell life insurance want you to buy *life insurance* to "pay for your long-term care", not long-term care insurance.

These life insurance policies are called "hybrids" and they are *very profitable* for the insurance companies. After working with thousands of consumers across the country, I know that hybrid policies are rarely the best way to protect your life's savings from long-term care expenses.

Throughout the book you'll find "K.E.Y." questions.

"K.E.Y." stands for:

Knowledge
Empowers
You

These "K.E.Y." questions will put you on equal footing with the insurance agent or investment advisor who is trying to sell you their product. These questions will help you cut-through the jargon and help you know which policies are lemons, and which policy will help you protect your life's savings.

Buying long-term care insurance is very different than buying other insurance products. You buy most insurance products many different times over the course of your life. Long-term care insurance, however, is a once-in-a-lifetime purchase. For many people, long-term care insurance is the capstone to their retirement plan. That's why it's important to take your time, educate yourself, consider all your options, and then *act!*

> You buy the same insurance products many times over your lifetime. Long-term care insurance, however, is a once-in-a-lifetime purchase. It's the capstone to your retirement plan.

CHAPTER 2

THERE ARE 5 TYPES OF INSURANCE POLICIES THAT CAN PAY FOR LONG-TERM CARE. WHICH ONE IS RIGHT FOR YOU?

To get the long-term care coverage that is right for you, you need to understand that there are five different types of policies. Which type of policy is best for you will depend upon several factors including:

- ➤ your age
- ➤ your state of residence
- ➤ your health history and
- ➤ your financial situation

Certain policies are better suited for certain ages.
Some policies are not available in every state.
Some policies have strict health requirements.
Some policies have lenient health requirements.
Some policies can protect your assets from Medicaid.

The five types of policies are:

1. traditional long-term care insurance,
2. long-term care partnership policies,
3. life insurance with a rider,
4. an annuity with a long-term care rider, and
5. recovery care policies.

We have a simple, web-based tool that can rank each type of policy for you. It's objective. It's instant. Click here to go to that tool or go to www.LTCShop.com and click on "Policy Finder".

Traditional

Long-term care insurance

Most things have improved over the past 25 years including long-term care insurance. Traditional long-term care insurance policies available for sale today have stronger consumer protections and better benefits than policies that were sold years ago.

Regulators enacted major reforms for long-term care insurance in 1993, 1996, 2000 & 2005.

However, insurance reforms are **NOT** retroactive. Insurance reforms are like airbags in cars. Airbags became mandatory for all new cars sold in the U.S. beginning on September 1st, 1998. The government regulations did NOT require that airbags be installed in older cars, only new cars.

The same is true for long-term care insurance. The long-term care insurance reforms implemented in 1993 did not improve policies purchased before 1993. The 1993 reforms only improved the policies that were purchased after 1993. The same is true for the reforms implemented in 1996, 2000, and 2005.

> In most states, long-term care insurance policies purchased today have all the consumer protections mandated by the 1993, 1996, 2000, and 2005 reforms.

Someone told me once that long-term care insurance policies were worthless because her father had dementia and his policy didn't pay anything for his care. She said his policy required a three-day hospital stay before it would pay benefits and his doctor wouldn't admit him into the hospital just because he had dementia. I replied that her father probably purchased his policy before 1993. She confirmed that he purchased his policy in the 1980's. I explained that her father's policy didn't have the 1993 reforms. His policy didn't have the "airbags" that are now required in every long-term care insurance policy.

Policies purchased today must:

- Cover all forms of dementia including Alzheimer's
- Cannot require hospitalization in order to qualify for benefits
- Cannot require that skilled care be needed in order to pay for custodial care
- Cannot require a prior nursing home stay in order to cover home care
- Underwriting must be done upfront. The insurer cannot do post-claims underwriting
- The insurer cannot cancel the policy for any reason (except if premium is not paid)

Long-Term Care Partnership Policies

The 2005 long-term care insurance reforms allowed all 50 states to create "Long-Term Care Partnership Programs."

"Long-term care Partnership" policies are special, government-approved policies that can help protect your assets from Medicaid even if your policy runs out of benefits. These policies can be very affordable because *you only need to buy an amount of insurance that is equal to the amount of assets you want to protect from Medicaid.*

"Long-term care partnership" policies have "dollar-for-dollar" asset protection. That means for every dollar your partnership policy pays in benefits, you can protect a dollar of your assets from Medicaid. Instead of having to spend down your savings to qualify for Medicaid, you can keep an amount equal to what your partnership policy paid in benefits.

Long-term care partnership policies are a special type of long-term care insurance.

- Every long-term care partnership policy is a long-term care insurance policy.

- Only some long-term care insurance policies are qualified to be long-term care partnership policies.

Most states have a long-term care partnership program. Click here to see if your state does. (Or go to www.LTCShop.com and click on "LTC Partnership".)

Life insurance
with some type of rider

An increasingly popular approach is to buy a life insurance policy with some type of a rider. The rider allows the life insurance policy's death benefit to pay for long-term care while you are alive. **This is the type of policy that most insurance agents and investment advisors sell to their clients today.**

These policies are commonly referred to as "hybrids". "Hybrid cars" combine a gasoline engine and an electric motor. "Hybrid policies" combine life insurance with a rider that is like long-term care insurance.

There are four different types of riders that can be attached to these life insurance policies. There are four different types of life insurance to which these riders can be attached. *It's VERY confusing. It's meant to be confusing.*

Most hybrid policies are a terrible way to plan for long-term care. A few hybrid policies are excellent.

The "K.E.Y." questions in this book will help you cut through all the "insurance jargon" so that you don't buy one of the lemons.

An annuity with
a long-term care rider

There are three types of annuities that are being promoted as "better alternatives" to long-term care insurance. Two of those annuities are expensive and inefficient ways to pay for long-term care. They are:

Deferred income annuities and
"Income doubler" annuities

> Do not use either of those types of annuities to plan for your long-term care needs. You're better off using your own money to pay for your care rather than one of those products.

For the purposes of planning for long-term care, there is only one type of annuity that can be very valuable. It is an annuity with a long-term care rider.

Essentially, it multiplies your single premium deposit for the purposes of long-term care. With some of these annuities the long-term care value is twice the single premium; with others it may be triple your single premium. If you pay for the inflation rider, your long-term care benefits can grow to five or six times the original premium deposit. If you never need care, your heirs will receive the cash surrender value.

However, this type of annuity is only a good idea if you can't qualify for a long-term care insurance policy due to age or health.

Recovery care policy

"Recovery care" policies are designed to pay benefits for shorter periods of time than long-term care insurance policies. "Recovery Care" policies will pay benefits for as short as 90 days and as long as two years, depending upon the policy and which options you choose.

Because "Recovery Care" policies have a much lower Lifetime Maximum than traditional long-term care insurance policies, they have much lower premiums than traditional long-term care insurance. "Recovery Care" policies are not approved for sale in every state.

When getting quotes for long-term care coverage ask each insurance agent or investment advisor the following "K.E.Y." questions:

> **K.E.Y. Question #1:** Which type of policy are you quoting for me? Traditional long-term care insurance, Long-term care partnership policy, Life insurance with a rider, Annuity with a long-term care rider, or a Recovery Care policy?

> **K.E.Y. Question #2:** Within the last two* years, have you taken the training required to sell long-term care partnership policies?**

*Connecticut, Indiana and New York only require that the training be taken one time, not every two years.

**The following states do not require any special training for insurance agents to sell long-term care insurance: Alaska, Hawaii, Illinois, Massachusetts, Mississippi, New Mexico, and Vermont.

CHAPTER 3

50% OF RETIREES SHOULD *NOT* OWN LONG-TERM CARE INSURANCE HERE'S WHY:

One-half of retirees do NOT need long-term care insurance because they can easily qualify for Medicaid-funded long-term care.

Medicare does NOT pay for long-term care beyond the first 100 days. Medicaid does.

> - You qualify for **Medicare** when you turn **65**.
> - You qualify for **Medicaid** only if your <u>income</u> **and** <u>assets</u> are below certain levels.

There are different rules for qualifying for Medicaid depending *if you are single or married*.

Medicaid for individuals

If you're single, to qualify for Medicaid-funded long-term care, you can have no more than $2,000 in "countable" assets. That figure may be slightly higher in some states. Additionally, all your income must go towards the cost of your care except for about $60 per month for "personal needs".

Medicaid for married couples

All assets are considered jointly held.

For married couples, Medicaid considers all assets as jointly held. The assets Medicaid considers are called "countable assets". Countable assets include all the following, in most states:

Savings accounts, checking accounts, money market accounts, certificates of deposit, retirement accounts (e.g. 401(k), 403(b), IRA's, etc...), stocks, bonds, mutual funds, treasuries, real estate investments, deferred annuities, cash value life insurance, pension plans, and assets in a revocable (living) trust.

If your and your spouse's countable assets are less than $247,200, you must spend down roughly half of your countable assets for one spouse to qualify for Medicaid.

If your and your spouse's countable assets are over $247,200, you must spend down all your countable assets to $125,600.

Income is considered separate.

While Medicaid considers all assets jointly held, Medicaid looks at each spouse's income separately.

Generally, all income of the spouse applying for Medicaid must go towards the cost of care (except for a small "personal needs allowance" of about $60 per month).

All income in the name of the healthy spouse can be retained by the healthy spouse. If the healthy spouse's income is less than $2,030 per month, the healthy spouse may be able to keep a portion of the other spouse's income. In some cases, the state may allow the healthy spouse to have monthly income as high as $3,090 per month.

When determining if Medicaid is the best option for a married couple, it's very important to understand Medicaid's income rules.

Can the healthy spouse afford to live on the income allowed by Medicaid?

If you buy long-term care insurance for only one spouse, which spouse should it be?

Clark was 67 when he decided to investigate long-term care insurance. His wife, Ellen, was almost 65-years-old. Clark was interested in buying long-term care insurance for his wife.

While explaining to him how Medicaid worked, I asked Clark to calculate their countable assets. He said they had countable assets of about $35,000. My first reaction was that they probably didn't need any long-term care insurance since they could pass Medicaid's "asset test" very easily. In their state, they would be allowed to keep all $35,000 and still qualify for Medicaid. They would not need to spend down any of their countable assets to qualify for Medicaid.

I knew he was an engineer with a Fortune 500 company for over 40 years. Since he had such a great career, I asked him why they didn't have more savings. He said they had nine children and he and Ellen put all of them through college, debt-free. (That explained it.)

We then discussed their income. Clark had a pension of $60,000 a year. It had a cost of living increase every year and Ellen would continue to receive his pension if he pre-deceased her. Clark also had about $15,000 a year in social security benefits.

Ellen had spent most of her adult life raising their children. After they were grown she worked long enough to earn a small pension of about $6,000 per year and social security benefits of about $9,000 per year.

Clark's income was $75,000 per year. Ellen's income was $15,000 per year. Their combined annual income was $90,000. Clark thought that since Ellen had less income than he that she should get long-term care insurance, not him. Just the opposite was true. Here's why:

For Ellen to qualify for Medicaid, the only requirement would be for her income to go towards the cost of her care. Clark could keep all his income if Ellen qualified for Medicaid. However, if Clark applied for Medicaid, almost all his income would go towards the cost of his care.

About $66,000 of Clark's $75,000 income would go towards the cost of his care. Ellen would have to live on the minimum amounts allowed by Medicaid (about $2,030 per month). I explained to him that he needed to protect his income from Medicaid so that Ellen could continue to live comfortably if he ever needed long-term care. He agreed and bought a policy for himself.

If Clark was buying a policy today I would recommend he buy a traditional long-term care insurance policy with a "cruise control" policy design (see chapter 8). Even at the age of 67, today he could purchase $500,000 of long-term care benefits for a monthly premium ranging between $230 and $340, depending upon his health and depending upon how much he was willing to co-insure. He could even buy a policy with an unlimited Lifetime Maximum.

There's a problem when relying

solely on Medicaid

Ellen didn't need long-term care insurance. She could qualify for Medicaid long-term care with only a minor impact on their household income. However, there are problems that can arise from relying solely on Medicaid to fund your long-term care.

HERE'S OUR MEDICAID STORY: Last year a relative of ours began having serious health problems. She lived about 1,300 miles from us. It was hard for my wife and I to manage her care from a distance and still run our business and raise our sons. We spent about six months trying to convince our relative to move closer to us and she finally agreed.

As soon as she gave us the OK we made all the plans. We scheduled the packers and moving van and we put her house up for rent. We started looking at facilities near us and we ran into a brick wall.

We were told there was a six to twelve month waiting list for the nursing facility closest to us. My relative was moving to our city in less than a month and we needed to find a place for her right away. We couldn't wait six to twelve months for her to move into a facility.

As a side note, we mentioned to the nursing facility administrator that our relative had a long-term care insurance policy that had a $10,000 monthly maximum. Once the administrator heard that, she told us there was no waiting list for our relative. Our relative could move into the facility right away. *The waiting list was only for those who were relying solely on Medicaid to pay for their care.*

> *Many good facilities that take Medicaid usually have long waiting lists for those who rely solely on Medicaid.*

Even though Ellen could qualify for Medicaid very easily, I would recommend that Ellen buy a "Recovery Care" policy. For about $94 per month, a 64-year old can get a "Recovery Care" policy that pays for one-year of care in a nursing facility. This makes it easier to get into a good facility quickly rather than being stuck on a Medicaid waiting list for months.

CHAPTER 4

THE TWO MOST IMPORTANT FEATURES IN EVERY TYPE OF LONG-TERM CARE COVERAGE.

When comparing the five types of policies the most important features to compare are the:

"MONTHLY MAXIMUM"
AND
"LIFETIME MAXIMUM"

The "Monthly Maximum" is the most your policy will pay for each month you need care.

The "Lifetime Maximum" is the most your policy will pay over your lifetime.

The Monthly Maximum is the most important part of any long-term care coverage. It's the first thing you should look at when comparing policies. The Monthly Maximum is very important because if it is too low you'll have to use your savings and/or income to make up the difference.

For example, if your care costs $10,000 per month but your policy's Monthly Maximum is only $4,000, you'll have to use your savings and/or income to pay the $6,000 difference **every** month you need care.

The Lifetime Maximum is especially important because you need to know when your policy might run out of benefits. This is especially important if you choose a long-term care partnership policy. Long-term care partnership policies provide protection for your assets even if your policy runs out of benefits.

When buying a long-term care partnership policy, you should match the policy's Lifetime Maximum with the amount of assets you want to protect from Medicaid. (See Chapter 7 for steps to design your long-term care partnership policy.)

It's NOT easy to compare.

It's not easy to compare the Monthly Maximum from one policy to the next. There is no standard terminology for the Monthly Maximum and each policy may call it something different.

Some long-term care insurance policies refer to it as a "Monthly Benefit".
Some long-term care insurance policies refer to it as a "Daily Benefit".

A few years ago I helped a couple shop for long-term care insurance. I found a perfect policy for them and sent them the paperwork to apply for it. After a couple of weeks, I hadn't heard back from them, so I called to see if they had any questions. They said they'd received a quote from their life insurance agent for a long-term care insurance policy that was a little cheaper and they were going to purchase that policy instead.

I asked them how much the Monthly Maximum was on that policy. They weren't sure at first, but they read from the illustration that the policy had a $3,000 "Monthly Benefit". The policy I recommended for them had a "Daily Benefit" of $150, which is comparable to a Monthly Maximum of $4,500. ($150 per day x 30 days = $4,500 per month)

A policy with a $3,000 Monthly Benefit sounded better to them than a policy with a $150 Daily Benefit. Fortunately,

> *I was able to explain it to them and help them avoid a big mistake.*

Comparing the Monthly Maximum becomes even harder when looking at a life insurance policy with a rider. Life insurance policies with riders determine the Monthly Maximum using an "Acceleration Rate". The Monthly Maximum is calculated by multiplying the life insurance policy's "Death Benefit" by the "Acceleration Rate". For example:

→If the "Death Benefit" is $100,000 and the "Acceleration Rate" is 4%, the Monthly Maximum is $4,000. ($100,000 x 4% = $4,000).

→If the "Death Benefit" is $100,000 and the "Acceleration Rate" is 2%, the Monthly Maximum is $2,000. ($100,000 x 2% = $2,000).

Both policies have the same $100,000 death benefit, but one would pay only $2,000 per month and the other $4,000 per month.

The following policies all have a $6,000 "Monthly Maximum":

→A long-term care insurance policy with a "Monthly Benefit" of $6,000.

→A long-term care insurance policy with a "Daily Benefit" of $200. ($200 x 30 = $6,000)

→A life insurance policy with a death benefit of $150,000 and an acceleration rate of 4%. ($150,000 x 4% = $6,000)

Regardless of which type of policy you are considering, ask the insurance agent or investment advisor this KEY question:

> **K.E.Y. Question #3:** If I need to use this policy in the very first year I own it, what is the maximum amount it will pay for each month I need care?

What about the future values?

The amount of the Monthly Maximum in the very first year you own your policy is very important. However, you probably won't need care the very first year you own your policy. You probably won't need care for many years down the road. Therefore, it's even MORE important to know how much the policy's Monthly Maximum will be in the years ahead.

A woman, in her mid-fifties, read something I had tweeted, and she contacted me asking for advice about a policy she had just applied for. She'd met with an insurance agent who showed her two different policies.

Each policy was nearly identical in price. One policy was a traditional long-term care insurance policy. It had a Monthly Maximum of $5,000 and a Lifetime Maximum of $250,000. The other policy was a life insurance policy with a rider. The death benefit could be used to pay for long-term care, if needed. It also had a Monthly Maximum of $5,000 and a Lifetime Maximum of $250,000. Since it was a life insurance policy, if she never needed long-term care, it would pay a death benefit of $250,000. Since the premiums were nearly identical it sounded to her like the life insurance policy was the better way to go.

She contacted me because she just didn't feel right about the choice; something was gnawing at her. I asked her, "What will the life insurance policy's Monthly Maximum be 5 years from now, 15 years from now, and 25 years from now?" She wasn't sure at first but after flipping through the pages of the illustration she noticed that the Monthly Maximum would always be $5,000. It didn't grow.

I then asked her to look at the quote the agent gave her for the traditional long-term care insurance policy. I asked her to check if the long-term care insurance policy included any type of inflation protection. If a long-term care insurance policy contains Inflation Protection the Monthly Maximum and Lifetime Maximum will grow every year automatically.

The quote the agent gave her for the long-term care insurance policy included a 3% compound Inflation Protection. That means the Monthly Maximum and the Lifetime Maximum would automatically increase every year by 3% compounded growth. With that policy the 3% compounded growth each year would not make the premium go up each year. The premium was designed to remain level, even though the benefits were guaranteed to grow every year.

Using a spreadsheet, I calculated for her how much the Monthly Maximum and the Lifetime Maximum would be in 5 years, 15 years, and 25 years (see chart).

The long-term care policy's Monthly Maximum and Lifetime Maximum would ***more than double*** over the next 25 years.

Two identically priced policies for a 55-year old, woman, in good health		
	Long-Term Care Insurance	Life Insurance w/Rider
Age 55 Monthly Maximum Lifetime Maximum	$ 5,000 $ 250,000	$ 5,000 $ 250,000
Age 60 Monthly Maximum Lifetime Maximum	$ 5,796 $ 289,818	$ 5,000 $ 250,000
Age 70 Monthly Maximum Lifetime Maximum	$ 7,789 $ 389,491	$ 5,000 $ 250,000
Age 80 Monthly Maximum Lifetime Maximum	**$ 10,468** **$ 523,444**	$ 5,000 $ 250,000

Her main reason for buying long-term care coverage was to be able to afford the best possible care, not leave money to an heir. A long-term care policy that grows by 3% compound every year would be better for her than a life insurance policy that didn't grow. She cancelled the life insurance policy and purchased a long-term care insurance policy instead.

The insurance agent she was working with should have explained to her that the long-term care insurance benefits would grow every year, but the life insurance policy wouldn't.

> **K.E.Y. Question #4:** When I need to use this policy, what is the maximum amount it will pay for each month I need care 5 years from now? 15 years from now? 25 years from now? Are these amounts guaranteed or are they just estimates?

> **K.E.Y. Question #5:** Does the "Lifetime Maximum" grow over time? If the "Lifetime Maximum" grows over time, how much will it be 5 years from now? 15 years from now? 25 years from now? Are these amounts guaranteed or are they just estimates?

The second part of the question is very important:
"Are these amounts guaranteed or are they just estimates?"

Many life insurance illustrations *estimate* the policy's future values. If the agent is showing you a life insurance policy with a rider, the future values may only be a projection and NOT guaranteed.

*Long-term care insurance policies, with inflation protection, have **_guaranteed_** future values.*

Some "experts" say that if you buy a long-term care policy you must get a 5% compound inflation benefit. That is not true. When comparing policies, focus on the future guaranteed values of the Monthly Maximum and the Lifetime Maximum. Do NOT focus on the percentage of growth. Here's why:

Two _**identically priced**_ policies for a 61-year old, single man, in good health		
	_3%_ Compound Inflation Protection	_5%_ Compound Inflation Protection
Age 61 Monthly Maximum	$ 6,000	$ 3,600
Age 66 Monthly Maximum	$ 6,955	$ 4,594
Age 76 Monthly Maximum	$ 9,347	$ 7,484
Age 86 Monthly Maximum	$12,562	$12,191

Even though these policies cost the same, the policy with the higher monthly benefit and a 3% compound inflation benefit provides richer benefits over a twenty-five-year period than the policy with a 5% compound inflation benefit. Years ago, 5% compound was "the best" inflation protection. Today, that is usually not the case.

CHAPTER 5

WHICH TYPE OF COVERAGE GIVES YOU THE MOST BANG FOR THE BUCK?

The best coverage for you is the

coverage that you can

Health-qualify for.

I know that sounds like I'm avoiding the answer, but it's true. Through no fault of your own you may have a health condition that prevents you from buying long-term care insurance. That's OK. If you can't qualify for a traditional long-term care insurance policy or a long-term care partnership policy, you may be able to qualify for a hybrid policy or a recovery care policy.

The healthier you are when you apply for long-term care coverage, the more choices you will have, and the lower your premium will be. That is why it's VERY important to investigate purchasing some type of long-term care coverage when you're healthy.

If you are healthy enough to qualify for any type of policy, which one will give you the most "bang for the buck"?

On the next page are two charts showing the amount of long-term care benefits $1 of annual premium can buy for a healthy 61-year old male and a healthy 61-year old female.

For $1 of annual premium, a 61-year old man can get about 5x as much long-term care benefits from a traditional long-term care insurance policy than he can get from a hybrid policy. Why? Because life insurance for a 61-year old man is expensive! Combining life insurance with long-term care insurance does NOT save money!

For $1 of annual premium, a 61-year old woman can get about 3x as much long-term care benefits from a traditional long-term care insurance policy than she can get from a hybrid policy. Life insurance for a 61-year old woman is not as expensive as it is for a man, but it is still a lot more expensive than a traditional long-term care insurance policy.

For $1 of annual premium a 61-year-old male, in excellent health, can buy:	
Amount of Long-Term Care Benefits	Policy Type
$207	long-term care partnership policy
$190	traditional long-term care insurance policy
$110	recovery care policy
$40	Life/LTC "hybrid" policy

For $1 of annual premium a 61-year-old female, in excellent health, can buy:	
Amount of Long-Term Care Benefits	Policy Type
$150	long-term care partnership policy
$163	traditional long-term care insurance policy
$110	recovery care policy
$53	Life/LTC "hybrid" policy

*These ratios were derived using policies which had $500,000 of long-term care benefits. The long-term care partnership policy would start off with $250,000 of long-term care benefits and grow to $500,000 by age 85.

If you read the Wall Street Journal, Kiplinger's, Morningstar, Marketwatch and most other "personal finance media", they are constantly writing this idiotic statement:

"If you don't want to buy an expensive long-term care insurance policy, you should consider buying a hybrid policy that combines life insurance with long-term care benefits." – BALONEY!

If long-term care insurance is too expensive why is the solution to spend three to five times MORE for a hybrid policy? It's illogical.

That's why I said at the beginning of this book: the insurance industry does NOT want you to buy long-term care insurance. The insurance industry wants you to buy life insurance instead; and *the insurance industry is using the "personal finance media" to mislead you.*

Recently I had an insurance agent challenge my statement that hybrid policies are three to five times more expensive than traditional long-term care insurance. He said he had recently compared a traditional long-term care insurance policy with a hybrid policy. The hybrid policy was only a "little bit" more premium than a traditional long-term care insurance policy.

His "client" was 51-years old and very healthy. He sold her a hybrid policy that had a $125,000 death benefit (which could be used for long-term care) and the premium was about $100 per month.

He was half-right. The hybrid policy was not three times as expensive as a comparable long-term care policy. The hybrid policy was about 50% more expensive than a comparable long-term care policy.

But, I asked him, "Why is she buying only $125,000 of benefits? The hybrid policy doesn't have any inflation growth. What good is $125,000 of benefits going to do for her 20 years from now? When she uses the $125,000 to pay for her care, she'll have to dip into her assets anyway?"

His answer floored me. He said, "That's all she could afford."

Smack my head!

I replied, "If her resources are that limited, wouldn't she be better off with a long-term care partnership policy? She could spend $100 per month and get a long-term care partnership policy that would include inflation protection AND protect her assets after the policy ran out of benefits."

Sometimes insurance agents can be more interested in the policy that is best for them to sell, rather than the policy that is best for you to own.

Another life insurance agent recently challenged me about this. He said he'd helped a 55-year old couple buy a million dollars of life insurance which could be used for long-term care. He said the life insurance policy was only about 10% more premium than a long-term care insurance policy, so they opted for the life insurance policy. I know how these policies are priced. I knew it couldn't be true, so I asked him to show me the quotes.

If you were going to compare a policy that had one million dollars of life insurance (which could be used for long-term care, if needed) wouldn't it seem logical to compare it to a long-term care insurance policy that also had one million dollars of benefits.

Well... he didn't do that. The long-term care insurance policy he showed them had a 5% compound inflation protection. The long-term care policy would grow to over four million dollars in benefits before they turned 85. If they lived to their mid-90's the long-term care policy would have over six million dollars in benefits.

The hybrid policy had no inflation protection.

It would never grow.

It would always have one million dollars in benefits.

If he'd done a more accurate comparison, the 55-year old couple could have purchased one million dollars of long-term care benefits for about one-third the cost of the life insurance policy he sold them.

CHAPTER 6

THE SIMPLE, LEGAL WAY TO PROTECT 100% OF YOUR LIFE'S SAVINGS FROM LONG-TERM CARE EXPENSES

"What if my policy runs out of

benefits?"

This is one of the biggest concerns with long-term care insurance. There are a few companies that sell long-term care insurance policies that have an unlimited Lifetime Maximum. When a policy has an unlimited Lifetime Maximum it can never run out of long-term care benefits no matter how long you may need care. However, policies with an unlimited Lifetime Maximum are usually very expensive. They are usually unaffordable for the middle-class.

To solve this dilemma, in 2005, the federal government passed legislation to allow all 50 states to develop a "Long-Term Care Partnership Program".

Click here to see if your state has implemented an LTC Partnership Program (or go to www.LTCShop.com and click on "LTC Partnership").

Each "Long-Term Care Partnership Program" encourages the middle-class to purchase an amount of long-term care insurance that is equal to the amount of savings they want to protect from Medicaid. If their long-term care policy runs out of benefits they can apply for Medicaid to pay for their care and their assets will be protected, both while they are alive and even after they pass away.

> *You can target how much long-term care insurance you need based upon how much of your assets you want to protect from Medicaid.*

If you want to protect more savings, you can buy more benefits for a higher premium. If you have less savings, you can buy less benefits for a lower premium. This program is an equitable and affordable solution for those who want to plan ahead.

"Long-Term Care Partnership Programs" give you "dollar-for-dollar asset protection". That means for every dollar your partnership policy pays in benefits, you can protect one dollar from Medicaid. Earlier I stated, "If your and your spouse's countable assets are over $247,200, you must spend down your countable assets to approximately $125,600." Here's how the Long-Term Care Partnership Program changes that:

Rick and Ilsa have $500,000 of countable assets. Rick falls off a ladder and is partially paralyzed from the injuries. He needs home health aides caring for him several hours every day. Before Medicaid will begin to pay for his care, Rick and Ilsa must spend down their $500,000 of countable assets to $125,600.

Fortunately, Rick and Ilsa don't have to spend down their assets. They bought a Long-Term Care Partnership Policy several years ago. They chose a starting Lifetime Maximum of $300,000. Their Lifetime Maximum has grown to $375,000 of benefits because of the inflation protection.

For every dollar their policy pays in benefits, they can protect one dollar from Medicaid. When their policy runs out of benefits Rick can apply for Medicaid and all their countable assets will be protected from Medicaid both now and even after Rick and Ilsa pass away.

It is called a "Long-Term Care *Partnership* Program" because it is a partnership between:

1. the federal government,
2. your state government,
3. select insurance companies,
4. specially-trained insurance agents,
5. and *YOU!*

The most important part is YOU!

The Partnership Program has been created for your benefit. But you must enroll ***while you are still healthy***. You've got to plan ahead.

CHAPTER 7

TWO SIMPLE QUESTIONS TO ASK WHEN CHOOSING THE BENEFITS IN YOUR LONG-TERM CARE PARTNERSHIP POLICY

"Long-term care insurance is too complicated!"

It's true. Long-term care insurance is complicated. Fortunately, the Long-Term Care Partnership Program has helped simplify it. When designing your long-term care partnership policy, you only need to ask yourself two questions to determine what benefits you should have in your policy:

1. How much of my assets do I want to protect from Medicaid? (for myself, for my spouse/partner, for my heirs, and/or for charity)
2. How much of my income can I comfortably allocate towards the cost of my care each month

and still keep all my other financial commitments?

The answer to the first question is the amount which you should target for your policy's Lifetime Maximum.

The answer to the second question will help you determine how much your Monthly Maximum should be. Find out the current cost of care in your area at this website, subtract how much you can comfortably allocate towards the cost of your care each month, and the result is what your Monthly Maximum should be.

Keep in mind that most people who need long-term care receive their care at home. There are only about 1.4 million people in nursing homes today, but there are about 11 million people who are receiving care at home. Home care is expensive, but it is much less than nursing home care.

What about a death benefit?

Long-term care partnership policies do NOT have a death benefit. Keep in mind that the policies protect your assets from Medicaid even after you die. The assets your partnership policy protects from Medicaid are essentially a death benefit for your heirs.

What about Inflation Protection?

Every long-term care partnership policy must include some type of inflation protection. After choosing your Lifetime Maximum and your Monthly Maximum, ask the insurance agent to give you a variety of quotes using different types of inflation protection. Ask the insurance agent to calculate the policy values 5 years from now, 15 years from now and 25 years from now.

CAUTION: Some types of inflation protection DO NOT qualify for the long-term care partnership program. Make sure each quote the agent gives you states specifically that it qualifies as a long-term care partnership policy.

Keep in mind, since the inflation benefit will cause your lifetime maximum to increase, you may want to start off with a smaller Lifetime Maximum than you think. A policy that starts off with $350,000 of benefits will grow to $500,000 in only 12 years if the policy has a 3% compound inflation protection.

A 5% compound inflation benefit is usually not the best choice.

It's important to understand that the cost of home care and nursing home care goes up each year, but it does not go up as fast as the cost of medical care. Medical costs increase each year due to the costs of research and development, expensive prescription drugs, and highly-paid medical personnel.

The cost of home care is based mostly on the cost of labor. Between 2013 and 2017 the home care inflation rate averaged only 2.50% per year. The nursing home inflation rate averaged only 3.76% per year.

In the 1980's, when long-term care insurance was still called "nursing home insurance" some regulators were sitting around a table one day discussing that these "nursing home policies" should include some type of inflation protection.

In the first half of the 1980's the inflation rate for every day expenses averaged about 7.5% **PER YEAR**. As they sat around the table they asked, "What percentage do you think we should require in these nursing home insurance policies?" Somebody said, "How about 5%?"

Voila! Ever since then every insurance company has to *offer* a 5% compound inflation protection to everyone who buys a long-term care policy.

> *In most cases you will be better off buying a higher Monthly Maximum with a lower inflation protection rather than a lower Monthly Maximum with a higher inflation protection.*

What about the Elimination Period?

The Elimination Period is the number of days you receive qualified care before your long-term care policy can begin to pay benefits. In most cases, you're better off with a 90-day Elimination Period rather than a shorter Elimination Period.

<u>Here's why:</u>

If you need rehabilitative care (e.g. physical therapy, speech therapy, etc...) most medical insurance policies (including Medicare and Medigap policies) can pay up to 100 days in a skilled nursing facility. With most of the better long-term care insurance policies, those days of care can count towards fulfilling your Elimination Period, even though you did not have to pay anything out-of-pocket for those 100 days of care.

If you need care due to a chronic illness (e.g. Parkinson's, arthritis, diabetes, dementia etc...), your care needs will probably start off slowly and you'll gradually need more and more care. Since you may need less care initially (for example you may only need a few hours of care each day for the first 90 days) your out-of-pocket expense for those first 90 days may be modest.

The shorter the Elimination Period, the higher the premium. If you're going to spend more premium you might be better off buying a higher Monthly Maximum rather than buying a shorter Elimination Period.

For example, a 30-day Elimination Period usually costs about 20% more premium than a 90-day Elimination Period. If you're going to spend 20% more premium you might be better off buying 20% more Monthly Maximum rather than a 30-day Elimination Period. In other words,

For about the same premium, would you rather have a policy that pays:

$5,000 per month starting on day 31
–OR–
$6,000 per month starting on day 91?

I'd pick the latter.

Also, keep in mind that federal law requires that a long-term care policy that meets the federal guidelines can only pay benefits when your care is expected to last 90 days or longer. If your doctor certifies that you are expected to recover in 89 days or less, a policy with a 30-day Elimination Period would not pay any benefits. The policy can only pay benefits if your doctor certifies that your care is expected to last 90 days or more.

> *Some long-term care insurance policies will allow care provided by a family member to count towards the Elimination Period.*

CHAPTER 8

TRADITIONAL LONG-TERM CARE INSURANCE VS. LONG-TERM CARE PARTNERSHIP POLICIES: WHICH IS BETTER FOR YOU?

If you're healthy enough to qualify for either a traditional long-term care insurance policy or a long-term care partnership policy, which one should you choose? It depends upon your income and your assets.

There are two ways to design a long-term care insurance policy:

- Pedal to the Metal and
- Cruise Control

"Pedal to the Metal" is designed to use up the policy benefits <u>as quickly as possible</u>. This is the ideal way to design a Long-Term Care Partnership Policy. The faster the policy benefits are paid out the faster you earn the "dollar for dollar" asset protection. Once the policy runs out of benefits you can apply for Medicaid and your savings will be protected.

"Cruise Control" is designed to cover most, ***not all***, of your long-term care expenses over a long period of time. There is usually no inflation protection in this type of policy design. Anyone buying a policy designed like this understands that they will have to use some of their income and/or assets to make up the difference between the future cost of care and the policy's Monthly Maximum. The goal of the "Cruise Control" policy design is so that your policy benefits last a very long time and prevent you from ever applying for Medicaid.

What's interesting about the following policy designs is that they are priced with nearly identical premiums, yet the benefits are very different.

Here's how these two different policy designs would look for a healthy couple, both age 61.

Year	*Pedal to the Metal* Monthly Maximum Lifetime Maximum Inflation Protection	**Cruise Control** Monthly Maximum Lifetime Maximum Inflation Protection
1	$5,000 $300,000 shared 3% Compound	$8,400 $1.5 Million shared None

5	$5,796 $347,782 shared 3% Compound	$8,400 $1.5 Million shared None
15	$7,789 $467,390 shared 3% Compound	$8,400 $1.5 Million shared None
25	$10,468 $628,133 shared 3% Compound	$8,400 $1.5 Million shared None
35	$14,069 $844,158 shared 3% Compound	$8,400 $1.5 Million shared None

Since both policy designs cost the same in premium, how do you decide which one is best for you? Our "Policy Finder" tool asks you a few questions and then instantly ranks each type of policy for you. If you haven't tried it yet, click here to try it out or just go to www.LTCShop.com and click on "Policy Finder".

Since long-term care partnership policies protect your assets, but do not protect your income, the lower your income the more sense a long-term care partnership policy makes.

The more comfortable you are using some of your own assets and/or income to put towards the cost of your care, the more you should lean towards the "Cruise

Control" policy design. The "Cruise Control" policy design is NOT a long-term care partnership policy because it does NOT have any inflation protection.

CHAPTER 9

A SIMPLER WAY TO COMPARE POLICIES

Before I explain a simpler way to compare policies, you must first understand a very important fact:

Insurance agents do not determine how much your long-term care insurance premium is.

The insurance companies set the premium.
The insurance agent does NOT set the premium.
The insurance agent canNOT change the premium.

If you buy X benefits from Y company, the premium will be the same regardless of which insurance agent you buy the policy from.

You might ask then, "If insurance agents don't set the premiums, what's the point of shopping around?" Here are several good reasons why you should shop around:

First, some insurance agents just don't understand long-term care insurance very well. You'll realize that after speaking with a few different agents.

Second, no insurance agent represents every company. If an insurance agent tells you that he/she represents every long-term care insurance company, he/she is lying.

Third, there are huge disparities in costs between companies. Some insurance companies charge twice as much as other companies, for the SAME benefits. Therefore, you need to shop around and get quotes from a variety of companies.

Fourth, some insurance agents might add extra riders to the policy that you don't need to increase the premium and thereby increase their commission.

Now, here's the simpler way to compare policies: **Pick your premium**

How much do you want to pay for long-term care coverage each month?

You decide.

Tell the insurance agents you're working with to give you a quote for $XXX per month of premium. Then tell the agents to calculate the two most important policy values (KEY questions #3 and #4).

Ask the agent, "If I pay $XXX per month, how much will the Monthly Maximum be in Year 5, Year 15, and Year 25 and how much will the Lifetime Maximum be in Year 5, Year 15, and Year 25."

Since all the policies the agent quotes for you will have the same premium, it'll be very easy for you to find the one that gives you the most "bang for the buck".

You may find that the premium you picked provides benefits that are much richer than you need. If that happens, ask the agent to re-calculate the quotes using a lower premium amount. If the agent you're working with isn't willing to provide you with new quotes and help you narrow down your best policy design, then find a better agent.

CHAPTER 10

THE SIMPLEST WAY TO COMPARE THE TOP LONG-TERM CARE INSURANCE POLICIES

The simplest way to compare the top policies is to work with a "long-term care insurance specialist". Unfortunately, there's no school to attend to become a "long-term care insurance specialist."

And there aren't very many of us.

Paying a $100 fee to join a "long-term care insurance association" does not make someone an expert on long-term care insurance. Even being "endorsed" by this association or that association doesn't mean the insurance agent is an expert on the topic.

Here's a few tips to help you find a "long-term care insurance specialist":

First, using your favorite search engine search on: "long term care insurance (your state)" or something similar. Read the website of several different insurance agents who offer long-term care insurance in your state. You'll probably have to read through the first 30 or 40 results to find 3 or 4 agents worth calling. *It's OK if the long-term care insurance specialist does not live in your state.* If they are licensed in your state and have completed your state's long-term care partnership training, that's all that matters.

> *It's OK if the long-term care insurance specialist does not live in your state as long as they are licensed in your state and have taken your state's long-term care partnership training.*

Second, if you find a website that does not have the name of the agent and the license numbers of the agent, **skip that website**. That website is probably a "lead-generating" website and will probably give your information to many different agents. You'll be inundated with phone calls and spam emails.

Third, after reviewing the websites written by real agents, you should contact three or four and "interview each agent". The #1 question to ask the agent is if he/she has taken the continuing education courses required to sell "Long-Term Care Partnership" policies in your state. If the agent is not qualified to sell a Partnership policy then the agent is severely limited in what policies he/she can offer. Many agents do not sell partnership policies due to the specialized training and continuing education requirements.

Fourth, ask the agent which companies he/she will quote for you. Ideally, the agent should provide you with a comparison of at least seven different policies.

Fifth, be prepared to answer several health questions when you speak with each agent. If the agent doesn't ask you health questions, that's a "red flag". The premiums are based upon your health history. The healthier you are the lower your premiums will be. If you're "not-so-healthy" your premiums will be higher. A "long-term care insurance specialist" will be familiar with each companies' health guidelines and will know which company is most likely to approve you with good rates. Be upfront with the agent about your health history. They can't share your health information with anyone else. By law they are obligated to protect your health information.

Lastly, do NOT work with an agent who expects you to make a quick decision. Choosing your long-term care coverage is a VERY important decision. It is a once-in-a-lifetime purchase and it is the capstone for most retirement plans. You should never feel pressured into applying for a policy after one phone call or one "on-line" meeting with an insurance agent.

CHAPTER 11

3 REASONS WHY INSURANCE COMPANIES LOVE IT WHEN YOU BUY A SINGLE-PREMIUM "HYBRID" POLICY

A "hybrid policy" is a life insurance policy that includes long-term care benefits. Many hybrids are sold as single-premium products. You don't pay premiums year after year. You make one large premium payment.

Insurance companies love it when consumers buy these single-premium products. Here's why:

1) <u>They earn money on your money for the rest of your life.</u>

You pay them a large lump sum and they earn money on your money for the rest of your life. Even though the policy may say you are earning 3% or 4% or more, when you look at the guaranteed cash value on the illustration the actual growth (***after fees***) is usually less than 1%. With some single-premium hybrid products the growth is NEGATIVE. The first reason NOT to buy a single-premium hybrid is that you lose out on all the money you could have earned if you'd kept the single-premium yourself.

2) <u>When you need care, the insurance company uses your money first.</u>

If, for example, the single-premium is $100,000, the insurance company uses that money to pay for your care FIRST before they use their own money. With most hybrids your single premium is used to fund the first 2 to 3 years of care. If the single-premium you pay is $100,000, essentially, you're buying a long-term care policy with a *$100,000 deductible*.

3) <u>When you need care, you'll have to use even more of your own money.</u>

Most hybrid policies have no inflation protection. A $100,000 single-premium hybrid policy for a 61-year old woman, would pay less than $6,500 for each month she needs care. Twenty years from now, if care is costing $14,000 per month, and the hybrid is paying only $6,500 each month, you'll have to use your own money to make up for the $7,500 shortfall each month.

Here's a Better Idea:

Wouldn't it be better to just keep the $100,000 yourself and earn what you can earn on it?

If you could earn 3.5% on a conservative mutual fund, you could earn enough each year to pay the annual premium of a well-designed long-term care policy that has inflation protection built into it.

→If you never need care, your heirs will get the $100,000 when you die.
→If you do need care, your heirs will still get the $100,000 when you die.
→You don't lose the $100,000 like you would with a hybrid.

If you buy a long-term care partnership policy, you can protect your assets from Medicaid even if your long-term care policy runs out of benefits.

If a hybrid policy runs out of long-term care benefits, it does not protect your assets from Medicaid.

(That is why when we do recommend hybrid policies we recommend hybrid policies that have an unlimited Lifetime

Maximum, which means it can never run out of long-term care benefits.)

Here's what happened with one of our clients:

Recently we helped a client of ours, age 69, obtain a long-term care partnership policy. He has $200,000 of countable assets that he wants to protect from Medicaid. He was able to purchase a long-term care partnership policy for less than $190 per month. If his long-term care partnership policy runs out of benefits, he can apply for Medicaid to pay for his care and all his countable assets will be protected.

Before making a final decision, he asked his life insurance agent about it. His life insurance agent said he wasn't a fan of long-term care insurance. The life insurance agent suggested he buy a single-premium hybrid policy with a $200,000 death benefit. The death benefit could be used for long-term care, if needed. The single-premium hybrid with a $200,000 death benefit would cost *$84,000.*

He was able to protect $200,000 of his countable assets with a long-term care partnership policy for less than $190 per month. Or, he could have paid $84,000 to get $200,000 of benefits from the single-premium hybrid.

If his long-term care partnership policy runs out of benefits, his assets **_will be protected_** from Medicaid. If the hybrid policy ran out of benefits, his assets would **_not_** be protected. It's a no-brainer.

CHAPTER 12

MANY "HYBRIDS" HAVE THESE PITFALLS THAT NO ONE IS TALKING

Hybrids are "OR" "OR" "OR", not
"AND" "AND" "AND"

Hybrid policies are sold as one policy that gives you three different benefits:

➢ "cash value" AND
➢ "long-term care benefits" AND
➢ "a death benefit"

However, you canNOT get all three benefits from the policy. You can only get one. If you buy a hybrid, you'll get:

✓ "cash value" **OR**
✓ "long-term care benefits" **OR**
✓ "a death benefit"

Hybrids are "If you use it, you lose it" policies.

If you use the cash value in the hybrid policy,
- *you lose* the long-term care benefits and
- *you lose* the death benefit

If you use the long-term care benefits in the hybrid policy,
- *you lose* the cash value and
- *you lose* the death benefit

If you're healthy a hybrid is usually three times the cost of a traditional long-term care policy, but you're NOT getting three times the benefits because ***if you use one of the benefits, you lose the other two.***

Many hybrids can lapse <u>even</u> if

you pay the premiums on-time

every year

Hybrids are sold as the best of all worlds with three different ways to benefit from the policy:

1) If you need cash, you can cancel the policy and get your cash.

2) If you need long-term care, you can use the death benefit to pay for your long-term care.

3) If you don't need long-term care, then your heirs will get the tax-free death benefit. OR

4) *you and your heirs could get NOTHING from the policy.*

Unfortunately, this is a very real possibility and it is rarely discussed.

Even if you pay your premiums on-time, every year, and NEVER miss a payment, the policy could lapse.

Not every hybrid, but many hybrid policies can lapse.

If the policy lapses, you will lose every penny you put into the policy.

If the policy lapses you will get NOTHING from the policy:

No cash value.
No long-term care benefits.
No death benefit.

Most hybrid policies are NOT guaranteed to stay in-force for the rest of your life. They might lapse when you reach age 90 or 85 or 80 or maybe even sooner than that. The only way to know that the policy will remain in-force for life is if you look at the page of the illustration that shows "guaranteed values". That page will show you the guaranteed death benefit every year of the policy. If the death benefit is zero before you reach age 100 that means you could lose everything you put into the policy and get NOTHING out of the policy. All your premiums would be wasted.

> **K.E.Y. Question #6**: If an insurance agent or an investment advisor is trying to sell you a hybrid policy ask, "What is the premium I must pay to guarantee that this policy stays in-force until my 100th birthday?" Then ask the agent to show you the page of the illustration with the "guaranteed premium" and the "guaranteed death benefit through age 100".

Low (or negative) interest rate

Hybrids are often advertised as crediting you with 4% interest (or a similar interest rate). However, after policy fees the actual interest rate is usually *negative.*

When you look at the illustration, go to the page that shows "Guaranteed Values". Then look on the column that says, "Cash Surrender Value". The "Cash Surrender Value" is what you'll receive if you cancel the policy. You'll see that the "Cash Surrender Value" is usually less than what you've put into the policy. With a few policies, the "guaranteed cash surrender value" may grow to be higher than the sum of your premium payments, but even then, the actual growth is usually less than 1%.

Long-term care insurance can pay benefits sooner

In 1996, the federal government created standards by which long-term care insurance policyholders would qualify to receive benefits. Every new policy today, that meets the federal guidelines, has three ways for the policyholder to qualify for benefits. Benefits are payable if the policyholder requires:

1) *"hands-on"* assistance to perform any two of the six* activities of daily living OR
2) *"stand-by"* assistance to perform any two of the six* activities of daily living OR

3) supervision to protect the policyholder's health and safety due to a cognitive impairment

*The six activities of daily living are: bathing, dressing, eating, toileting, getting out of a bed or chair, and maintaining continence.

I have a close relative who is in an assisted-living facility. She has a long-term care insurance policy that meets the federal guidelines. A few times each week she needs "hands-on" assistance to help with bathing. Every morning and every night she needs "stand-by assistance" to change her clothes. She has problems with balance. Dressing and undressing requires a lot of balancing. She needs someone within arm's reach to make sure she doesn't fall and injure herself while she's changing her clothes.

Most hybrid policies use "chronic illness" riders. "Chronic illness" riders do not have to meet the federal guidelines for long-term care insurance. In particular, "chronic illness" riders do not include "stand-by" assistance as a means for the policyholder to qualify for benefits. If my relative had a hybrid policy with a "chronic illness" rider she would not be receiving any benefits from the policy because she needs "stand-by" assistance with one of the activities of daily living. Fortunately, she has a long-term care insurance policy that meets the federal guidelines and the policy is covering the full cost of the assisted-living facility.

Most hybrid policies are like Swiss army knives!

Most hybrid policies are like Swiss Army knives: they can do more than one thing, but they don't do any of them very well. When you go to wrap a birthday gift do you grab your Swiss Army knife and pull out the tiny little scissors to cut the wrapping paper? Of course not. You get a real pair of large, sharp scissors.

If you need long-term care, you'll get significantly better benefits, for much less premium, with a traditional long-term care insurance policy rather than a hybrid policy.

There is no such thing as a hybrid policy that has excellent cash value growth, and an excellent death benefit, and excellent long-term care benefits.

- As far as an investment, most hybrids give very little (or no) return on your money.

- As far as a death benefit, most hybrids give a very small death benefit in comparison to the amount of premium you pay.
- As far as long-term care benefits, most hybrids have much lower long-term care benefits than a traditional long-term care insurance policy.

If your main goal is cash value growth, don't buy a hybrid! Invest your money in something that will grow.

If your main goal is a death benefit, don't buy a hybrid! You can usually get a much higher death benefit for less premium if you buy a life insurance policy that is not a hybrid.

There are some hybrids that have EXCELLENT long-term care benefits, but very little cash value growth and a very small death benefit. If your main concern is planning for long-term care and you want to buy a hybrid, buy a hybrid that has great long-term care benefits and ignore the cash value and the death benefit.

But what if I need life insurance AND I need long-term care insurance? Shouldn't I buy a hybrid?

If you need life insurance, do NOT

buy a hybrid.

Buy two separate policies.

With a hybrid, if you need long-term care for a long enough period, you lose most (usually all) of the death benefit.

If you need life insurance and you need long-term care insurance, you should NEVER buy a hybrid; buy two separate policies. In many cases, my clients can get better long-term care benefits and better life insurance benefits, FOR LESS PREMIUM, if they buy two separate policies rather than buying one hybrid policy.

CHAPTER 13

WHAT IF YOU CAN'T QUALIFY FOR LONG-TERM CARE INSURANCE OR A HYBRID?

If you can't qualify for a long-term care insurance policy, then you should consider a hybrid policy. If you can't qualify for a hybrid policy, then you should consider an annuity with a long-term care rider.

There are three types of annuities that are being promoted as "better alternatives" to long-term care insurance.

> *Two of these are a terrible way to plan for long-term care. They are: Deferred income annuity and "Income doubler" annuity.*

A deferred income annuity requires a large, lump sum premium payment and then generates monthly income for you beginning at some future date. There are two main problems with using this type of annuity to plan for long-term care. The first problem is low interest rates. To generate enough income to pay for even part-time home care you'd have to deposit a very large sum of money into the annuity. The second problem is that you don't know when you'll need long-term care! You must set your income date in advance, usually 10 or more years into the future. What if you need long-term care before then.

An "income doubler" annuity is an annuity that pays you a monthly income, but if you need long-term care the monthly income doubles. That sounds great until you look at the numbers. The monthly income generated by the annuity is very small in comparison to the amount of money you put into it.

> When planning for long-term care, there is one type of annuity that can be very valuable: **An annuity with a long-term care rider.**

An annuity with a long-term care rider

Essentially, this type of annuity multiplies your single premium deposit for the purposes of long-term care. With some of these annuities the long-term care value is twice the single premium deposit. With others the long-term care value is triple the single premium deposit. If you buy the inflation rider, the long-term care value can grow to five or even six times the original premium deposit.

With most of these annuities your single premium deposit is used to pay for the first 24 months of care. With some of these annuities your premium is used to pay the first 30 to 36 months of care.

If you die without needing care, your beneficiary receives the cash value of the annuity. If you need a little bit of care and use some of the deposit, your beneficiary will receive the balance of the cash value of the annuity.

This type of annuity is a terrible investment. The cash value grows by less than 1%. In most cases there is zero growth in the cash value. With some of these annuities the cash value decreases every year.

The reason for owning this type of annuity is to build a hedge around your other assets to protect against a lengthy period of care. Your single premium deposit is used to pay for your first 24 to 36 months of care (depending upon the policy). The real value in this annuity comes after you've used the single premium deposit to pay for your care. Then the long-term care rider kicks in and the insurance company starts to use their money to pay for your care.

To make this type of product worthwhile, it requires a large single premium deposit, usually no less than $100,000. This type of annuity is only a good idea for someone who can't qualify for a traditional long-term care insurance policy due to age or health reasons AND has at least $500,000 of investable assets (excluding home equity).

Since you're using your single premium deposit to pay for the first 24 to 36 months of care, the underwriting requirements on this type of annuity are *very lenient.* *You can have a lot of health problems but still purchase this type of annuity.*

CHAPTER 14

IF YOU DECIDE TO BUY A "HYBRID" MAKE SURE IT HAS THESE FEATURES!

Fully guaranteed benefits.

If you are considering buying a hybrid policy, you should only buy a hybrid policy that has:

    1. A death benefit that is **_guaranteed through age 100_** and

    2. A long-term care benefit that is at least twice as much as the death benefit

First, the death benefit must be guaranteed through age 100. (The best hybrids guarantee the death benefit through age 120).

This is vitally important. If the death benefit is not guaranteed through age 100 then you could pay your premiums for years but end up:

- losing all the death benefit AND
- losing all the long-term care benefits AND
- losing all the cash value.

Here's how to find out if the death benefit is guaranteed through age 100:

If an insurance agent or investment advisor is trying to sell you a hybrid policy, ask them to give you the complete illustration. It will be at least 10 pages long. Find the page in the illustration that shows, "Guaranteed Values". That's the ONLY page that matters.

The far-left column of the page should be titled "Insured's Age". Follow that column down the page until you reach the row where the age is 100. Follow that row all the way over to the far-right column entitled, "Death Benefit". Make sure the "Death Benefit" is at least as rich at age 100 as it is the first year of the policy.

If the "Death Benefit" at age 100 is zero,
don't buy that policy.
There are better policies out there with better guarantees.

Second, the long-term care benefits should be at least twice as much as the death benefit. If you buy a hybrid policy that has long-term care benefits that equal the death benefit, you are not getting any leverage. You are overpaying.

The best hybrid policies have <u>unlimited</u> long-term care benefits.

CHAPTER 15

5 REASONS TO BUY LONG-TERM CARE INSURANCE INSTEAD OF A "HYBRID"

If you're healthy enough to qualify for long-term care insurance, you're better off buying a long-term care insurance policy rather than a hybrid for five reasons:

1. More benefits for each dollar of premium
2. Federally-mandated consumer protections
3. Protection of assets from Medicaid
4. Tax-deductible premiums AND tax-free benefits
5. Specially-trained insurance professionals

First, you'll get more long-term care benefits for a lot less premium from the long-term care insurance policy. (see Chapter X) Hybrids cost a lot more than long-term care insurance because every hybrid has a death benefit. If your main concern is planning for long-term care, you'll get more long-term care benefits for less money with a long-term care insurance policy rather than a hybrid.

Second, you'll get federally-mandated consumer protections when you buy a long-term care insurance policy. Most hybrids do not have these consumer protections because most hybrids do not meet the federal requirements for long-term care insurance. For example, with a long-term care insurance policy you have the right to have your policy reinstated up to five months after it has lapsed if you had a cognitive impairment at the time the policy lapsed. Most hybrids do not give you the federally-mandated consumer protections.

Third, hybrid policies do not protect your assets from Medicaid. If your hybrid policy runs out of benefits you'll have to use your own assets to pay for your care and then go on Medicaid. With a long-term care partnership policy you can protect your assets from Medicaid even if your policy runs out of benefits. (For our clients who can afford it we often recommend a hybrid policy that has an unlimited Lifetime Maximum. This hybrid can never run out of long-term care benefits.)

Fourth, long-term care insurance policies that meet the federal guidelines have tax-deductible premiums AND tax-free benefits. Only two types of insurance have tax-deductible premiums and tax-free benefits: long-term care insurance and medical insurance. Hybrids do not have tax-deductible premiums because hybrids are life insurance and life insurance is not tax-deductible. (There is one hybrid where a portion of the premium is tax-deductible.)

Fifth, only specially-trained insurance agents can sell long-term care insurance and long-term care partnership policies. To sell long-term care insurance and especially long-term care partnership policies, insurance agents are required to take special training and update their training every two years. Any insurance agent can sell a hybrid policy. No special training is required to sell a hybrid.

CHAPTER 16

YOU MAY NOT WANT TO BUY YOUR LONG-TERM CARE COVERAGE FROM...

- ➢ Investment advisor
- ➢ Auto & home insurance agent
- ➢ Someone who has the name of one insurance company on their business card
- ➢ An association (e.g. professional, alumni, retirement, etc.)
- ➢ Your employer

... from an investment advisor.

Investment advisors are licensed to sell securities as well as insurance products. However, investment advisors can only offer insurance products that are approved by the investment firm they work for. There are thirteen different companies that sell traditional long-term care insurance. There are several companies that sell good hybrid policies. An investment advisor is probably allowed to sell for two of these companies, maybe three.

Ask your investment advisor to provide you with quotes from the two or three different companies they use for hybrids and long-term care insurance. Don't assume that any of those policies are the best choice for you. *Your investment advisor is showing you those policies because those are the policies approved by the investment firm.* They may be good policies, but <u>they may not be the best for you</u>.

... from your auto or home insurance agent.

Most auto and home insurance companies don't sell long-term care insurance. If the company you use for auto and home insurance sells long-term care insurance, you should get a quote. You should be able to get a quote right over the phone. It doesn't cost you anything to get a quote from them.

Recently I was tweeting with someone who said long-term care insurance was too expensive. I asked her how she came to that conclusion. She said she'd gotten a quote from her auto and home insurance agent and the premium was $2,000 *per month*. I asked her the name of the company and I opened my software which contains the premiums for about 12 different companies. I ran a few quotes from other companies and let her know that she could buy a half million dollars of long-term care benefits for about $200 per month.

I'm not sure why her home and auto agent thought it would be a good idea for someone to spend $2,000 per month on long-term care insurance. Get a quote from your home and auto insurance company, but make sure you compare it with quotes from other companies.

... from someone who has the name of one insurance company on their business card.

When I first started out in the insurance business I was a "career agent" with John Hancock. John Hancock's name and logo were on my business card. I was able to sell policies from other companies, but I was "strongly encouraged" to only sell John Hancock policies.

Also, I had a quota. I had to sell so many John Hancock policies every quarter to keep my medical insurance and my retirement benefits. If an insurance agent has the name of a specific insurance company on their business card, ask them to give you a quote for that company. Keep in mind, that agent has an obligation to sell that company's policy. Don't assume that policy is the best one for you. Make sure you get other quotes, talk to other agents, and shop and compare.

... through an association

Associations offer lots of different benefits to their members, including insurance. Many associations offer "discounted" long-term care insurance rates to their members.

> Be careful of "association discounts" when buying long-term care insurance.

A few months ago, a couple went to my website and filled out my "Quote Request Form". Five years ago, they purchased a "discounted association policy" through the husband's alumni association and now they wanted to compare rates.

The insurer that was endorsed by the association gave a 10% discount to all the members of the association, including their spouses. Because of the 10% discount, they assumed it was a good deal, and they signed up right away without taking the time to compare other policies.

> Discounts are intended to entice you to buy now without taking the time to shop around.

The policy offered by their association was a good policy. It had a starting Monthly Maximum of $4,500. It had a starting Lifetime Maximum of $270,000. It had 3% Compound Inflation Protection so that their benefits would grow every year. If they'd taken the time to shop around, I could have gotten them a policy from a company with higher financial ratings and better benefits, for about $900 per year less (per person).

> Don't assume that your association has done the shopping for you!!!

Get a quote from your association, but then compare it with other policies before making your final decision.

... through your employer.

One of the most common mistakes people make when buying long-term care insurance is to assume that group long-term care insurance is better. Conventional wisdom says that group insurance policies cost less than a policy you purchase on your own. That is true for some types of insurance, but it is not always true for long-term care insurance.

If you're very healthy, especially if you're married, you may be able to get better benefits for less premium if you purchase your own policy rather than enrolling in a group long-term care policy.

A few years ago, I helped a couple purchase long-term care policies. A few months later they called and said they were going to cancel their policies because their employer was now offering a group long-term care policy. They assumed that the group policy was going to be better than the policy they'd purchased on their own. I encouraged them to take a close look at the group policy and to carefully compare the features of the group policy with the features in their individual policies.

Here's what they found out:

- ✓ The group policy had the same Monthly Maximum for facility care, but the group policy paid 25% LESS for care received at home.
- ✓ The group policy had a Lifetime Maximum of $273,500. The policy they bought on their own had an unlimited Lifetime Maximum.
- ✓ Even though the group policy had less benefits, it cost 15% MORE premium than the policy they purchased on their own.
- ✓ What was even more surprising was that the group long-term care policy was offered by *the exact same insurance company* from whom they had purchased their individual policies.

The same insurance company gave better benefits and charged less premium for individually-purchased long-term care policies, rather than group long-term care policies. Why? Because group policies usually don't give discounts for being married (individual policies do). And group policies usually don't give discounts for good health (individual policies do).

If your employer offers a group long-term care insurance policy, get a quote, but make sure you compare it to several individual policies with benefits that are similar to the group policy.

CHAPTER 17

WATCH OUT: SOME POLICIES HAVE PREMIUMS THAT GO UP EVERY YEAR. LOOK FOR THESE CLUES.

K.E.Y. Question #7: As the benefits increase each year, will the premium increase each year?

There are two types of Inflation Protection:
  A. The benefit increases each year do NOT make the premium go up each year.
  B. The benefit increases each year DO make the premium go up each year.

These two types of Inflation Protection are often confused because the wording in the brochures can be very similar.

Here is an example of language that is sometimes used to describe "Type A": "Your Daily Benefit will automatically increase by 5% compound every year."

Here is language that is sometimes used to describe "Type B": "Every year you will be offered the opportunity to buy additional coverage. Your Daily Benefit will increase by 5% compounded annually."

> It's a subtle difference. Buying additional coverage means your premium will go up.

Recently, I was helping a couple shop for long-term care insurance. They were given a quote for a long-term care policy by an insurance agent from whom they had purchased life insurance.

The policies had the same Monthly Maximum and the same Lifetime Maximum. The only difference between my quote and the life insurance agent's quote was the Inflation Protection. The life insurance agent represented a company that sold a long-term care policy that had a "Type B" Inflation Protection. ***Every year their premium would go up unless they kept their benefits level.***

My quote, on the other hand, had a "Type A" Inflation Benefit. The 5% increases in the benefits each year would not make the premium go up each year.

They'd assumed that their life insurance agent had found them the best deal because the quote was lower. After I explained the difference to them they calculated the future premium increases and realized they'd be better off with the policy that had the Type A Inflation Benefit.

Don't get stuck with a policy that has a "Type B" inflation benefit. Be sure to ask the insurance agent KEY Question #7: "As the benefits increase each year, will the premium increase each year?"

Here's how the policies would differ in cost over the years:

Year	Daily Benefit	Policy Limit	Premium Inflation Type A	Premium Inflation Type B
1	$170	$372,300	$4,174	$3,310
5	$207	$453,002	$4,174	$4,022
10	$264	$578,160	$4,174	$5,134
15	$337	$738,030	$4,174	$6,552
20	$431	$945,094	$4,174	$8,364
25	$552	$1,208,880	$4,174	$10,064

CHAPTER 18

THE SIMPLEST WAY TO GET A LONG-TERM CARE INSURANCE CLAIM APPROVED *FAST!*

There are FIVE things that make long-term care insurance claims hard to file. Fortunately, there's one trick which I have personally used that make the long-term care insurance claims process super easy. First, here are the five things that make it hard:

1. No Prior Experience – The hardest part about a long-term care insurance claim is that it's brand new for everyone. Even though over one million people have received benefits from their long-term care policies, most of us have never filed a long-term care insurance claim. Your doctor has lots of experience filing medical insurance claims, but probably no experience filing long-term care insurance claims.

2. Medical Records – Before approving a claim, the insurance company needs to review the policyholder's medical records. To prevent medical records from getting into the wrong hands, privacy laws have created roadblocks which are designed to protect you. These same roadblocks, however, can cause delays in getting your medical records from your doctor's office to the insurance company's claims department.

3. Legal Documents – The policyholder is usually not the one submitting the claim. If a relative of the policyholder is submitting the claim the doctor's office needs to know the relative has the legal authority to represent the policyholder. Until the doctor's office is satisfied that you have legal authority to represent the policyholder, they can't send any records to the insurance company.

4. "Snail Mail" – Most communication with the insurance company must be done via "snail mail" or over the phone. Sending health information via unsecure fax or email is a potential HIPAA violation subjecting the insurance company to huge fines. This can add to the frustration and delay the approval process even longer.

5. 60-day Deadline – Lastly, insurance laws in most states require the insurance company to either approve or deny the claim within 60 days from the date they received the claim form. If the medical records have not been received within that time, the claim must be denied. The claim can be re-opened once the medical records are received, but the claim denial letter that is sent on Day 60 causes a lot of confusion and makes an already stressful situation even worse.

Here's the Simple Trick...

When my relative decided to file a claim on her long-term care policy I did NOT handle her claim for her. Even though I'm a licensed insurance agent and I've specialized in long-term care insurance for over 20 years, I didn't handle her claim.

We contacted one of the largest home care agencies and they handled it for us. This home care agency processes *thousands* of long-term care insurance claims every year. All my relative had to do was sign a couple of HIPAA forms and the home care agency took care of the rest.

The agency handled the claim for free. It makes sense. They wanted to earn our business and get us to hire them to provide home care for my relative. They have a financial incentive to set up a system to quickly process long-term care insurance claims. It worked well for both parties. They got our claim approved quickly and easily and they provided home care to my relative until she moved into the assisted-living facility.

> *When shopping for long-term care insurance, it makes sense to work with an expert: a long-term care insurance specialist. When filing a long-term care insurance claim, it makes sense to work with an expert: one of the larger home care agencies.*

CHAPTER 19

ISN'T IT BETTER TO SELF-INSURE? CAN YOU EARN 25% ON YOUR INVESTMENTS EVERY YEAR?

A healthy, 61-year old man can buy a half million dollars of long-term care insurance for about $212 per month. Where could he invest $212 per month and turn it into $500,000? He'd have to earn 25% per year (pre-tax), every year, <u>for 20 years in a row.</u> Warren Buffett couldn't do that.

But that's not the biggest problem with self-insuring. The real problem is that no one knows the two most important variables in the equation. How can you successfully self-insure if you don't know:

1) when you will need care? and
2) for how long you will need care?

If you know you'll need care for 3 years, starting 30 years from now, then you could calculate exactly how much you needed to invest each month. But what if you need care for 5 years starting 10 years from now? Or, what if you need care for 9 years, starting 7 years from today?

> *Zack and Paula had just retired. She was in her mid-fifties and he was in his late sixties. They had worked hard and saved, and they were ready to enjoy a long, well-deserved retirement. Shortly after Paula turned 60, Zack was diagnosed with early onset Alzheimer's.*
>
> *What should she do? Should she deplete their retirement accounts paying for his care each month? Should she give up horseback riding and all the things she loved to do in order to be his 24/7 caregiver. What impact would that have on her own health?*
>
> *Fortunately, 7 years before he was diagnosed they purchased long-term care insurance. Over the past 9 years his policy has paid over $650,000 in benefits.*
>
> *Their retirement accounts are doing what they were meant to do: generate a retirement income which they won't outlive.*
>
> *Their long-term care insurance is doing what it was meant to do: protect their income streams.*
>
> *She is very happy her husband did **not** say, "Honey, maybe we should just invest this $3,800 each year instead of paying for this insurance?"*
>
> *They've already received a **2400% return** on the premiums he paid over that 7 year period.*

> *Instead of being his caregiver, she oversees his caregivers. Instead of deciding which asset to liquidate next, all she has to do is send the bill to the insurance company every month.*

- ➤ Investments are not a substitute for insurance.
- ➤ Insurance is not a substitute for investments.

- ➤ Invest well to ensure financial independence.
- ➤ Insure well to protect financial independence.

Would you risk hundreds of thousands of dollars for four-tenths of 1%?

Let's suppose you have a million dollars in your portfolio. Would you choose between well-diversified investments that were safe and earned, on average, 5.0% per year? Or would you choose riskier investments, which could lose hundreds of thousands of dollars, but they could earn you 5.4% per year?

A safe investment with a 5.0% return?

OR

A risky investment with a 5.4% return?

> ➤ The safe investment generates $50,000 per year from the $1,000,000 portfolio.
> ➤ The risky investment generates $54,000 per year from the $1,000,000 portfolio.

Which one would you choose?

Any reasonable person would choose the safe investment. The extra four-tenths of one percent is not worth risking hundreds of thousands of dollars.

The safe investment with a 5.0% return is the portfolio that is protected by long-term care insurance. Instead of risking the loss of hundreds of thousands of dollars in long-term care expenses, you re-allocate four-tenths of 1% each year, which pays for your long-term care policy, which then protects your principal. Doesn't that make sense?

Which asset will you liquidate first?

One of the problem's with "self-insuring" is that there's usually not a plan put in place before the need for care arises. Not everyone needs or wants long-term care insurance, but everyone should have a long-term care plan. If you're going to self-insure then you need to have a heart-to-heart conversation with your family and say, "If I need long-term care, use my assets to pay for the care. Liquidate this asset first, then this one, then this one, etc...."

I was having a conversation with a gentleman who said he was going to self-insure for long-term care because he had enough money to pay for the care. So, I asked him:

Have you and your spouse made a list of which assets to liquidate in what order?

Have you specifically told your children to use your assets to pay for your care instead of becoming your caregivers?

He said there was no need to liquidate any assets because his annual income was $120,000 and that was higher than the most expensive nursing home in his area. I asked:

If you need long-term care, will all your other expenses stop?

Doesn't your wife also rely on that $120,000 per year? What will she live on?

He didn't want to think about that so he answered, "I'm willing to take that risk."

I know what it's like to be a caregiver and the havoc it can bring on a family when no plan is in place. So, I replied:

You're not putting yourself at risk.
You're putting your family and loved ones at risk.
They are the ones who will bear the burden of your care, not you.

Even though he said he was going to self-insure, what he was really saying was, "I don't want to think about it."

For the sake of your loved ones, you need to think through these hard questions.

Not everyone needs (or wants) long-term care insurance.

But everyone should have a long-term care plan.

Your long-term care plan starts with the answers to three basic questions:

✓ Where will you receive your care?
✓ Who will provide the care?
✓ How will the care be paid for?

What if someone has $10,000,000? Should they own long-term care insurance?

Let's assume that a married couple, in their late fifties, has $10,000,000 of assets which they have invested in a well-diversified portfolio. They have a home worth $900,000 and there's no mortgage. After giving to their favorite charities each year, the dividends and interest they earn on their investments cover the full cost of their living expenses. Most years they can re-invest some of their investment returns. Through capital appreciation and re-investing their portfolio grows every year.

They have a one-million-dollar umbrella liability policy that costs them $1,000 per year. The $1,000 per year premium is less than two-tenths of 1% of their annual income.

Since they have ten million dollars in their portfolio should they cancel the one-million-dollar umbrella liability policy?

The smart answer is: "They should keep the umbrella policy."

People who are smart with their money and their investments live by this maxim:

"watch the downside and the upside will take care of itself."

It makes sense to hedge against a potentially large loss by spending only $1,000 per year on the umbrella policy. The same is true for long-term care insurance.

A healthy couple in their late fifties could buy about $1.5 million of long-term care insurance benefits for a combined annual premium of $4,000.

The $4,000 per year premium is .04% of this couple's net worth.

The $4,000 per year premium is less than 1% of this couple's annual income.

It makes sense to hedge against the potentially large loss by spending only $4,000 per year.

> *After running the numbers, the more money someone has the more sense it makes to own some long-term care insurance.*

CHAPTER 20

HOW DO I KNOW THE INSURANCE COMPANY WILL PAY MY LONG-TERM CARE CLAIM WHEN I GET OLDER? I'LL BE TOO SICK TO FIGHT THEM.

It's true that many of the older long-term care insurance policies had provisions that restricted access to benefits. Many of the older policies would only pay benefits if you first had a three-day hospital stay. Some older policies would not pay for care resulting from Alzheimer's. Some policies would only pay for home care if you needed "skilled care" at the same time. Many older policies only covered nursing homes and wouldn't pay benefits for care received in assisted-living facilities.

The federal government and state insurance regulators outlawed these restrictive provisions in the mid-1990s for all new policies, but not the old policies. In 2010, the federal government commissioned an audit of the seven largest long-term care insurers to see how well these new laws protect policyholders at the time of claim. They concluded that the claims were being paid and the consumer protections were working.

A more recent study by America's Health Insurance Plans, in 2014, found that only 4 percent of claims had been denied. Claims are denied when the policyholder does not meet the federal guidelines for benefit eligibility. Of the 4% who were initially denied, nearly half of them (1.6%) were approved once they did meet the federal guidelines for benefit eligibility.

But the easiest way to get your long-term care insurance claim approved is to have a large home care agency submit the claim for you. Most of them do it for free because they want you to become their client.

CHAPTER 21

IF A COMPANY STOPS SELLING LONG-TERM CARE INSURANCE POLICIES WILL IT PAY MY CLAIM IN THE FUTURE?

It is true that most of the insurance companies that sold long-term care insurance in the 1990's no longer sell long-term care insurance. It's also true that most of the insurance companies that sold medical insurance in the 1990's don't sell medical insurance anymore.

Over the past 20 years, to reduce overhead expenses and achieve economies of scale, the insurance industry, like most industries, has consolidated. Many of the companies that sold medical insurance merged with other companies that sold medical insurance. Many of the companies that sold long-term care insurance merged with other companies that sold long-term care insurance.

> *Last year over 100 different insurance companies paid claims to their long-term care insurance policyholders.*

All the companies that have stopped selling new long-term care insurance policies are still paying claims on their old policies. They have no choice! **They are legally obligated to pay all claims.**

Last year over 100 different insurance companies paid claims to their long-term care insurance policyholders. You can view the LTC insurance claims data in a report published annually by the National Association of Insurance Commissioners.

CHAPTER 22

IF THE LONG-TERM CARE INSURANCE COMPANY GOES BANKRUPT WILL MY CLAIM BE DENIED?

If an insurance company goes bankrupt the state guaranty associations step in to help pay the claims. Check out www.nolhga.com to learn more.

Every state has a guaranty association to make sure that claims are paid when an insurer goes through financial difficulty. State guaranty associations have maximum benefit levels that can vary from state to state, but most provide coverage of up to at least $300,000 in long-term care insurance policy benefits.

Over the past 40 years there have been roughly 150 different insurance companies that have sold long-term care insurance policies. Three of those insurance companies went through liquidation. All three of those insurance companies were very small with financial ratings that were well BELOW average. Combined those three companies had less than a 2% market share of LTC insurance policies.

It's important to buy all types of insurance from financially-sound insurance companies, especially long-term care insurance. Always check the financial ratings of any insurance company you are considering. As a service to our clients, we provide links to the most current financial ratings of all the insurance companies we quote for them.

CHAPTER 23

SIMPLIFYING FINANCIAL RATINGS: WHAT YOU SHOULD LOOK FOR AND WHAT YOU SHOULD IGNORE

There are many different agencies that rate insurance companies for their financial strength. They all use different criteria and different ranking systems. It's intended to confuse you. Here's all you need to know:

The two most important rating agencies are A.M. Best and S & P. Ideally you want to buy your long-term care coverage from a company that is ranked at least "A minus" by A.M. Best and S & P.

You should ignore the "Comdex" composite. In my opinion, the Comdex is easily misunderstood, by both consumers and insurance agents. The Comdex is not a rating, it's a percentile using the ratings from the ratings agencies.

Here's how the Comdex can be easily misunderstood:

Suppose I'm a freshman in college and I take "Microeconomics 101". I take the mid-term exam and get 90% of the questions correct. A 90% is excellent. I got 9 out of every 10 questions correct. My professor gives me an "A minus". However, half my classmates scored higher than a 90. The other half scored lower than a 90.

If Comdex was my professor, Comdex would give me a "50", not a "90". Comdex would give me a 50 because 50% of my classmates scored lower than I did and 50% of my classmates scored higher than I did.

That's why I think the Comdex composite can be misleading. A company can have a strong financial rating (e.g. an "A minus") and still get a low Comdex rank. Unfortunately, when consumers look at the Comdex rankings they equate a Comdex rank of "50" with a failing grade.

The other problem with the Comdex composite is that many insurance companies are not ranked by all the ratings agencies. Comdex gives a lower percentile to an insurance company if it has only 2 ratings, even if those ratings are excellent.

CHAPTER 24

YUGO FAILED!
LONG-TERM CARE INSURANCE
MUST BE DEAD NOW.

Between 1985 and 1992, over 140,000 Yugos were imported into the United States. The Yugo rarely met emission standards, had an unreliable electrical system, and continually broke down. The joke went:

"Why does the Yugo come with a rear defroster?"
"So your hands stay warm when you push it."

Needless to say, when Yugo pulled out of the U.S. market, no one was surprised, and no one cared. Yugos accounted for less than 1% of auto sales.

Did the headlines read, "Collapse of Yugo Reveals Deep Problems Plaguing the Auto Industry?"

Of course not. No newspaper would have written such a ridiculous headline. Yugo's failures were caused by Yugo's mismanagement.

After a small long-term care insurance company was ordered by the court to be liquidated, the Wall Street Journal headline read, "Collapse of Long-Term Care Insurer Reflects Deep Industry Woes."

Penn Treaty was a small LTC insurance company with about 1% of the market share and below average financial ratings. Penn Treaty is not an example of the entire long-term care insurance industry, just like Yugo is not an example of the entire auto industry.

The writer of the article, Leslie Scism, did a good job of explaining how long-term care insurers mispriced their policies in the 1990's and early 2000's. However, her article failed to point out the real reason for Penn Treaty's demise. Penn Treaty's mistakes went well beyond mispricing.

Penn Treaty's failure was caused by them designing and selling policies that did not meet the federal guidelines for long-term care insurance.

The federal government recommends, and the rest of the long-term care insurance industry uses, "Activities of Daily Living" to determine when a long-term care policy will pay benefits. The six Activities of Daily Living are: bathing, dressing, eating, toileting, transferring, and maintaining continence.

Penn Treaty used "*Instrumental* Activities of Daily Living" to determine when a policy will pay benefits. The "*Instrumental* Activities of Daily Living" are: meal preparation, shopping, light housekeeping, laundry, using the telephone, and bill paying.

Penn Treaty is the only insurance company to use "*Instrumental* Activities of Daily Living" to determine when benefits will be paid. Clearly it didn't work. Thankfully, no other company has made that same mistake nor ever will.

CHAPTER 25

DOES THE AVERAGE LONG-TERM CARE POLICY COST $5,000 PER YEAR?

In 2015 Marketwatch published an article stating: "A 55-year-old couple buying one common long-term care policy today can expect to spend a little more than $5,000 a year on premiums."

> *Including all rate increases, the average long-term care insurance premium is $1,591 per year, based on data published in 2015 of all seven million LTCi policies in-force.*

Because of new consumer protections designed to prevent future rate increases, policies purchased today cost more than older policies. In 2015, the average premium for a new policy was $2,532 per year, according to a LIMRA survey of most companies selling long-term care insurance.

But don't base your decision about long-term care insurance on "averages" because some companies charge 80% more than others!

If you pay an "average" premium, you're overpaying for long-term care insurance and you didn't work with an agent who could help you shop around and compare policies.

Each insurance company has a very different way of pricing their long-term care policies based upon your age, your health and your choice of benefits. The difference in pricing from one company to the next is *astonishing.*

> ➤ Example #1: A healthy, 61-year old single male, can get $500,000 of long-term care insurance benefits for $212 per month. Or, that same healthy 61-year old single male can get $500,000 of long-term care insurance benefits for $391 per month. *Same coverage. Two different companies.*

> ➤ Example #2: A healthy, 61-year old couple can share $500,000 of long-term care insurance benefits for $134 per month per spouse. Or, that same healthy 61-year old couple can share

$500,000 of long-term care insurance benefits for $283 per month per spouse. *Same coverage. Two different companies.*

That's why it's very important to get quotes from many different companies when shopping for long-term care insurance. If the agent you're working with does not show you actual quotes from at least seven different companies, find another agent.

> *Why would some companies charge 80% more premium than other companies?*

The higher-priced companies may have higher distribution costs or higher overhead expenses or higher profit margins. It's probably a combination of all three.

CHAPTER 26

DIDN'T ONE LTC INSURANCE COMPANY NEARLY QUADRUPLE MONTHLY PREMIUMS OVER THE PAST TWO YEARS?

In March 2016, Kaiser Health News published an article about a 69-year old woman whose "monthly premiums have nearly quadrupled over the past two years."

Long-term care insurance rate increases are public information. I knew the article contained inaccurate information. No long-term care insurance company has ever quadrupled its premiums over 20 years, let alone over 2 years. To double check I contacted the woman who was the subject of the article and she confirmed how much her premiums had increased.

Her premiums did NOT "nearly quadruple" over a two-year period. Over a 17-year period, everyone in

California who purchased the same policy she purchased had a 13 percent increase, a 41.6 percent increase and a 58.6 percent increase.

It is true that this is one of the largest cumulative increases of any long-term care policy ever sold. (It averages out to about 9% per year.) However, to say that her premium "nearly quadrupled over the past two years" is false. I contacted the writer of the article and shared the facts with her. She said that she'd double check her notes and get back to me. She never has.

Unfortunately, the article failed to mention that the State of California, and 40 other states, have passed regulations to help prevent large premium increases. The woman who is the subject of this article bought her policy about three years before California passed that regulation, so her policy is not protected by California's Rate Stability Regulation.

CHAPTER 27

WHY AREN'T THERE ANY REGULATIONS TO PROTECT ME FROM PREMIUM INCREASES?

It is true that many of the older long-term care insurance policies have had large premium increases. Fortunately, insurance regulators today do not allow the new long-term care policies to use the old pricing methods.

> *To prevent rate increases, 41 states have enacted very strict pricing regulations for new policies.*

For an insurance company to get approval to sell a new long-term care insurance policy today, the policy must comply with the following pricing regulations:

- ✓ It must be priced higher than all previous policies that company has ever sold in that state,
- ✓ It must include ALL prior rate increases in the pricing, and

✓ It must include a pricing "cushion" (about 10%) as extra protection from rate increases.

For example, if the older policy sold by the insurance company cost $1,000 per year for X benefits and that policy had an 80% rate increase, a new policy with X benefits must be priced no less than $1,980. Here's how that's calculated:

$1,000 (older policy pricing)
plus 80% (older policy rate increase)
plus 10% (cushion)
= $1,980 (new policy pricing)

Now this is bad news and good news. The bad news is that a policy purchased today costs more than a similar policy that was purchased 10 years ago. The good news is that since today's policies are priced very carefully you are less likely to have a large premium increase in your lifetime.

New Rules Have Removed the
Profit Incentive from Rate
Increases

To discourage rate increases even further, regulators in 41 states have removed the profit incentive from long-term care insurance rate increases. Under the old rules, when a rate increase was requested the insurance company could include their regular profit levels into the rate increase. In many cases, a rate increase resulted in larger profits for the insurance company.

Under the new rules, if an insurance company requests a rate increase they must decrease the profit levels in their pricing to a cap that is pre-determined by this new regulation. They must re-allocate those former profits towards claims payments which results in a lower overall rate increase. Lastly, they cannot price profit into the rate increase itself, only a small amount for administrative costs.

The 41 states that have implemented this new rule have seen fewer and smaller rate increases on long-term care insurance.

> *Unfortunately, many group policies (like the Federal Long-Term Care Insurance Program, CalPERS, and other self-funded groups) do not have to comply with these new pricing   regulations.*

CHAPTER 28

WAITING TO PLAN FOR LONG TERM CARE UNTIL YOU NEED CARE, IS LIKE WAITING TO SAVE FOR RETIREMENT UNTIL YOU RETIRE.

Waiting to plan for long-term care until you need care, is like waiting to plan for retirement until you retire--it doesn't work!

You can't get hurricane insurance for your house when there's a tropical storm warning. Once the storm is coming, it's too late to get the insurance. You can't get collision insurance for your car after you drive into a telephone poll. Once the accident has happened, it's too late to get collision insurance.

You can't get long-term care insurance after you've broken a hip and need a walker for the rest of your life. You can't get long-term care insurance after you've had a paralyzing stroke and need a quad cane for the rest of your life. You can't get long-term care insurance once you've been diagnosed with Parkinson's or Alzheimer's or Multiple Sclerosis or Mild Cognitive Impairment, because the storm is on the horizon and it's headed straight for you.

There are a lot of reasons to own long-term care insurance. The last few pages of this book are not my words. These next few pages are words from real people, just like you, who own long-term care insurance. These real people share the reasons why they decided to buy long-term care insurance.

> "In terms of wealth, we are in the middle, and I believe the insurance can be of considerable value if needed. I don't consider the payments wasted if they are never used... Instead, I consider the insurance a gift to my spouse and kids."

> "It seems to me that one of the more meaningful considerations to keep in

mind in regard to LTC insurance is that it assures coverage of some of the most important aspects of quality-of-life during the most dependent and vulnerable period in a person's adult life."

"The best reason I have heard for buying LTC insurance is so that your kids don't have to agonize over whether or not to get you the care you need, which might otherwise cost them their inheritance. Who would want to put that trip on his or her kids?"

"This is about money, but it is also about family consideration. Those who have had parents and had to struggle to take care of them while trying to take care of their own family and work at their jobs know that maintaining an ailing elderly parent can be a very challenging situation mired with guilt, weariness and financial strain for those who are trying to help. I do not want to put that all on my family. I see this insurance as money well spent to have the coverage if I need it."

"Just like life insurance, LTC insurance is not for the person who is insured – that person will get care no matter what. LTCi protects the family and more importantly, the spouse. Have you ever seen an 85-year-old woman trying to take care of an 87-year-old man who can't get himself bathed and dressed? Even if she could care for him, doing this day after day will soon take a toll on her health. Kids can help but usually only for a limited time."

"There is also a selfish aspect of my thinking. If I need care, I don't want my wife to scrimp (on my care). There should be no reservations about using the insurance coverage, as opposed to spending down assets. I am also not well equipped to provide all the care for my wife, if say, she has a stroke and can't take care of herself."

"I have found solace for our decision (to own LTC insurance) by realizing that we have attempted to protect each of us from a potentially financially ruining situation... I don't disagree the odds of such an event are low, but this is the type of risk meant for insurance: low probability high impact."

"My policy will cover approximately two-fifths of the cost of a local good care facility......Now, you might ask what good is a two-fifths benefit; well, my income sources (SS, RMDs, annuity) will just about make up the other three-fifths, and if I need more, then I start dipping into my IRA balances. But our state has a partnership in place whereby I'd be able to retain assets in the amount of the total lifetime benefit if I needed to apply for Medicaid. This is very attractive to me, as I hope to leave at least a small legacy for my children."

"We didn't think the policies would cover the entire cost of care if we end up in a nursing home, but we thought between the policies and our savings, if one of us had to go into a nursing home we would be able to pay without impoverishing the other. The policies were not expensive (we bought them when we were in our early 50s and we're paying a little over $100 a month each for the coverage) and we feel like we are hedging our bets by having them."

"If you are having a hard time justifying the few thousand a year for the insurance you are in for a big "justifying" moment when you're asked for the $60,000 to $300,000 annual payments (to the home care agency or nursing home). Do you have a better plan?"

"I always look at insurance as the base of the investment pyramid. We decide what insurances are worth having to preserve all the assets stacked up on top of it. Then we let a portion of those assets pay for those insurances. We look at it as the cost of doing business, as they say."

68209081R00086

Made in the USA
Columbia, SC
05 August 2019